ASOGWA JUSTINA

Whispers of the Almighty

Copyright © 2024 by Asogwa Justina

All rights reserved. No part of this publication may be reproduced, stored or transmitted in any form or by any means, electronic, mechanical, photocopying, recording, scanning, or otherwise without written permission from the publisher. It is illegal to copy this book, post it to a website, or distribute it by any other means without permission.

Asogwa Justina asserts the moral right to be identified as the author of this work.

Asogwa Justina has no responsibility for the persistence or accuracy of URLs for external or third-party Internet Websites referred to in this publication and does not guarantee that any content on such Websites is, or will remain, accurate or appropriate.

First edition

This book was professionally typeset on Reedsy.
Find out more at reedsy.com

Contents

1	The Silent Messenger	1
2	The Hidden Scripture	5
3	The Unseen Hand	9
4	The Chosen Ones	14
5	The Sacred Seal	18
6	The Prophet's Dilemma	23
7	The Divine Conspiracy	27
8	The Last Covenant	32
9	The Whispering Shadows	37
10	The Judgment	42
11	The Veil of Deception	47
12	The Eternal Echo	52
13	The Judgment	57
14	The Whispering Shadows	62
15	The Final Revelation	67
16	The Silent Messenger	72

1

The Silent Messenger

The town of Havenbrook had always been a place where life moved slowly. Nestled in a valley surrounded by dense forests and rolling hills, it was a sanctuary of tranquility. Its residents were simple folk, their lives intertwined through generations of shared history and community bonds. The most exciting events were the annual harvest festival and the occasional out-of-town visitor. But all that changed one autumn evening when a stranger arrived, cloaked in mystery and whispers of the divine.

The first person to see him was old Mrs. Thompson, who lived alone in the last house on Maple Street. She was sitting on her porch, knitting a scarf for her grandson, when she noticed a figure emerging from the forest's edge. The man was tall, dressed in a long, dark coat that billowed around him in the evening breeze. His face was obscured by the wide brim of a hat, casting a shadow that seemed to swallow the fading light.

Mrs. Thompson watched as he walked with purpose down the road, pausing only once to glance around as if taking in his surroundings. His movements were smooth, almost ethereal, and for a moment, she felt a chill run down her spine. She shook her head, dismissing the unease as an old woman's fancy, and returned to her knitting.

The stranger continued his journey into the heart of Havenbrook, his presence unnoticed by most as they went about their evening routines. It wasn't until he reached the town square, where the statue of the town's founder stood proudly, that people began to take note. The square was bustling with activity as children played and parents chatted, but a hush fell over the crowd as he approached the statue.

He stopped at its base, looking up at the bronze figure with an intensity that drew the townsfolk's attention. Conversations ceased, and curious eyes turned towards him. The stranger raised his hand and pointed to the statue, his voice low but carrying a weight that demanded silence.

"I bring a message," he declared, his voice cutting through the evening air like a knife. "A message from the Almighty."

Gasps of shock and murmurs of disbelief rippled through the crowd. The man's claim was audacious, bordering on blasphemous in the eyes of some. Who was this stranger to speak for God? And why had he come to their quiet town?

Reverend Jameson, the town's pastor, stepped forward, his expression a mix of skepticism and concern. "What is this message you claim to bring?" he asked, his voice steady but wary.

The stranger turned his gaze towards the reverend, his eyes piercing and dark. "The Almighty has spoken to me," he replied. "And I am here to deliver His words. Change is coming. Prepare yourselves, for the days ahead will test your faith and your resolve."

The reverend frowned, his mind racing. "And why should we believe you? Many have come before, claiming to speak for God, only to lead people astray."

The stranger nodded, as if expecting the question. "You will believe, not because of my words, but because of what is to come. Watch for the signs, and you will see the truth."

With that, he turned and walked away, leaving the townsfolk in stunned silence. He disappeared into the night, his presence lingering like a shadow over Havenbrook.

The days that followed were filled with unease and speculation. Who was the stranger? Where had he come from? And what did his message mean? The people of Havenbrook were divided. Some dismissed him as a madman or a charlatan, while others felt a strange pull, a sense that something significant was indeed on the horizon.

Mrs. Thompson couldn't shake the feeling of foreboding that had settled over her since that evening. She found herself watching the forest edge, expecting to see the stranger reappear at any moment. Her nights were restless, filled with dreams of darkness and whispers she couldn't understand.

Reverend Jameson, too, was troubled. He spent long hours in his study, poring over scriptures and praying for guidance. He felt the weight of his responsibility to his congregation, and the stranger's words echoed in his mind. Was this a test of faith, as the stranger had suggested? Or was it a deception, meant to lead them away from the true path?

A week passed, and the town began to settle back into its routine, the stranger's visit fading into memory. But just as life seemed to return to normal, the first sign appeared.

It was a Sunday morning, and the townsfolk had gathered at the church for service. The pews were filled with familiar faces, all wearing expressions of reverence and anticipation. Reverend Jameson stood at the pulpit, preparing to deliver his sermon, when a sudden hush fell over the congregation.

A young boy, no more than ten years old, stood at the back of the church, his eyes wide with fear. "Fire," he whispered, his voice trembling. "There's a fire at the mill."

Panic erupted as the words sank in. The mill was the lifeblood of Havenbrook, its operation crucial to the town's economy. Without it, many would lose their livelihoods. People rushed out of the church, their faces pale with fear and dread.

When they reached the mill, they found the boy's words to be true. Flames licked at the wooden structure, smoke billowing into the sky. The townsfolk worked frantically to extinguish the fire, forming a human chain to pass buckets of water from the river. Despite their efforts, the fire raged on, relentless and unforgiving.

As they battled the blaze, a figure appeared on the hill overlooking the mill. It was the stranger, his coat and hat unmistakable. He watched silently, his presence once again sending a chill through those who saw him.

Reverend Jameson, covered in soot and sweat, looked up at the hill and saw the stranger. A sense of dread filled him, and he knew in his heart that this was the first sign the man had spoken of. The test had begun, and the people of Havenbrook were caught in the grip of a divine mystery that would change their lives forever.

2

The Hidden Scripture

The fire at the mill left Havenbrook in a state of disarray. As the days passed, the townsfolk worked tirelessly to rebuild, their faces etched with worry and determination. The stranger's ominous words lingered in their minds, casting a shadow over their every move. Little did they know, the fire was just the beginning.

One evening, as the sun dipped below the horizon and the sky turned a deep shade of crimson, Father Benedict, the elderly caretaker of the St. Augustine Monastery, was preparing for his nightly prayers. The monastery, perched on a hill overlooking Havenbrook, had stood for centuries as a beacon of faith and solitude. Its stone walls held countless secrets, the most profound of which were about to be unearthed.

Father Benedict moved through the dimly lit corridors, his footsteps echoing softly against the cold stone floors. He reached the chapel, its high arched windows casting long shadows in the fading light. Kneeling before the altar, he bowed his head in silent prayer, seeking guidance and strength in these troubling times.

As he prayed, a faint, almost imperceptible sound reached his ears. It was a soft whisper, like the rustling of ancient parchment. He lifted his head, straining to hear. The sound seemed to come from beneath the chapel floor, growing louder with each passing moment. His heart quickened, a mixture of fear and curiosity compelling him to investigate.

Father Benedict rose slowly, his joints protesting with age. He retrieved a lantern from the altar and lit it, the warm glow illuminating his path. He made his way to the back of the chapel, where a small, forgotten door led to the monastery's crypts. These crypts were seldom visited, housing the remains of monks who had long since passed.

He hesitated for a moment, his hand trembling on the iron handle. Taking a deep breath, he pulled the door open, the hinges creaking in protest. A chill gust of air greeted him as he descended the narrow staircase, the flickering lantern casting eerie shadows on the walls.

The crypts were silent, save for the whispering sound that had now grown louder, filling the space with an unsettling presence. Father Benedict walked slowly, his eyes scanning the rows of stone sarcophagi and cobweb-covered relics. His lantern's light fell upon an old wooden chest, half-buried in the corner. It was unlike anything he had seen before, its surface intricately carved with symbols and runes.

He approached the chest cautiously, his heart pounding in his chest. The whispering grew louder, almost deafening now. With trembling hands, he reached for the lid and lifted it. Inside, he found a bundle of ancient scrolls, their edges yellowed with age. The whispering ceased abruptly, replaced by a heavy silence that seemed to press down on him.

Father Benedict carefully removed the scrolls, his hands shaking with anticipation. He unrolled one, revealing text written in a language he did not recognize. The symbols seemed to dance and shift before his eyes, as if alive with hidden power. He knew at once that these were no ordinary writings. They were something far more significant, something divine.

With a sense of urgency, he carried the scrolls back to his study, locking the crypt door behind him. He spent the entire night poring over the ancient texts, trying to decipher their meaning. The more he read, the more he realized that these scrolls contained prophecies and revelations, messages that spoke of a time of great upheaval and divine intervention.

The next morning, Father Benedict summoned Reverend Jameson to the monastery. The young pastor arrived, his face etched with concern. The events of the past weeks had taken a toll on him, and he was eager for any news that might shed light on the stranger's message.

Father Benedict met him at the entrance, his expression grave. "Come with me, Reverend. There is something you must see."

They walked together to the study, where the ancient scrolls lay spread out on the desk. Reverend Jameson's eyes widened as he took in the sight. "What are these?" he asked, his voice barely above a whisper.

"These," Father Benedict replied, "are scriptures from a time long forgotten. They contain prophecies that speak of our present times and the trials we are to face. I believe they are connected to the stranger's message."

Reverend Jameson leaned in, studying the scrolls closely. "Can you read them?"

"Not entirely," Father Benedict admitted. "But I recognize some of the symbols. They speak of a coming darkness and a light that will rise to challenge it. There are instructions, too, though they are not clear. We must decipher these texts if we are to understand what is to come."

As the two men worked together, deciphering the scrolls by the dim light of the lantern, a sense of urgency grew within them. They knew that time was running out, and the fate of Havenbrook hung in the balance.

Meanwhile, in the heart of the town, rumors began to spread. People spoke in hushed tones about the fire, the stranger, and now the mysterious scrolls found in the monastery. Fear and suspicion grew, and the once tight-knit community began to fray at the edges.

In the dead of night, as Father Benedict and Reverend Jameson continued their work, a shadowy figure watched from the edge of the forest. The Silent Messenger had not left Havenbrook. He lingered, observing, waiting. The next sign was coming, and with it, the true test of the town's faith and resolve.

The whispers of the Almighty were growing louder, and soon, all would be revealed.

3

The Unseen Hand

The discovery of the ancient scrolls sent ripples of fear and curiosity through Havenbrook. As Father Benedict and Reverend Jameson worked tirelessly to decipher the texts, the town buzzed with speculation. Whispers of impending doom mingled with hope for divine intervention, creating an atmosphere thick with anticipation and dread.

In the heart of Havenbrook, life continued with an uneasy normalcy. The mill workers resumed their labors, rebuilding what the fire had destroyed. Children played in the streets, though their laughter was tinged with a nervous energy. Shopkeepers conducted their business with one eye on the door, half expecting the mysterious stranger to reappear at any moment.

One afternoon, as the sun cast long shadows over the town square, a peculiar event unfolded. Mrs. Harrington, the local grocer, was stacking shelves when she noticed a flicker of light from the corner of her eye. Turning, she saw a figure in the reflection of the shop's window. It was the stranger, standing motionless in the square, his presence as unsettling as ever.

She gasped, dropping the can she held. The clatter drew the attention of her husband, who came rushing from the back room. "What's wrong, Mary?" he asked, concern etched on his face.

She pointed to the window, her voice trembling. "He's back."

Her husband followed her gaze and saw the stranger. Without a word, he stepped outside, joining the growing crowd that had gathered around the square. The townsfolk watched in silence as the stranger raised his hand, pointing towards the church steeple. His voice, though soft, carried across the square with an eerie clarity.

"The Almighty's hand is upon you," he intoned. "Look to the skies, and you will see His power."

As he spoke, dark clouds began to gather overhead, swirling ominously. The air grew heavy, charged with electricity. A murmur of fear spread through the crowd. Then, as if on cue, a brilliant flash of lightning split the sky, followed by a deafening clap of thunder. The ground shook, and the church bell began to toll, though no one had pulled the rope.

Panic erupted. People scattered, seeking shelter from the sudden storm. The stranger remained unmoved, his eyes fixed on the sky. As the storm intensified, the town's power went out, plunging Havenbrook into darkness. Only the intermittent flashes of lightning illuminated the chaos.

In the monastery, Father Benedict and Reverend Jameson worked by candlelight. The storm had not escaped their notice, and they exchanged worried glances. "We must hurry," Father Benedict urged. "Time is running out."

Reverend Jameson nodded, his eyes scanning the scrolls. "There's a passage here," he said, pointing to a section of text. "It speaks of a great storm, a test of faith. Those who believe will find the strength to endure."

As they deciphered more of the texts, a pattern began to emerge. The prophecies foretold a series of trials, each more harrowing than the last, designed to test the faith and resolve of the people. They realized that the storm was just one of many signs to come.

Outside, the storm raged on. The town square was deserted, save for the stranger, who stood like a sentinel amidst the tempest. His eyes seemed to glow with an otherworldly light, and those who dared to look at him felt a chill that pierced their very souls.

At the edge of the forest, a young woman named Emily watched the scene unfold from her hiding place. She had been out gathering herbs when the storm hit and had sought refuge among the trees. Her heart pounded in her chest as she watched the stranger, her mind racing with questions. What did he want? Why was he here? And what did his presence mean for Havenbrook?

Emily had always been curious, her inquisitive nature leading her to explore the world beyond the town's borders. She had read about ancient prophecies and divine interventions, but never had she imagined witnessing such events firsthand. Determined to uncover the truth, she decided to follow the stranger, keeping to the shadows as he moved through the storm.

As the stranger walked, the storm seemed to follow him, the lightning and thunder mirroring his every step. He led Emily to the edge of the forest, where he stopped and turned his gaze upward. She held her breath, hiding behind a tree, and watched as he raised his hands to the sky. A bolt of lightning struck the ground before him, illuminating a hidden path that wound deep into the forest.

Emily hesitated, fear warring with curiosity. But the desire for answers won out, and she stepped onto the path, following the stranger at a distance. The forest was dark and foreboding, the storm above casting eerie shadows on the ground. She moved cautiously, her senses heightened, every rustle of leaves and snap of a twig sending her heart racing.

The path led to a clearing, where the stranger stood before an ancient stone altar, its surface covered in moss and vines. He placed his hands on the altar and began to chant in a language Emily did not recognize. The air around him shimmered, and the ground trembled as if responding to his call.

Emily watched in awe and fear, her mind struggling to comprehend what she was witnessing. She knew she had stumbled upon something far greater than she could have imagined, something that could change the fate of Havenbrook forever.

Suddenly, the stranger stopped chanting and turned towards her, his eyes locking onto hers. "You should not be here," he said, his voice filled with a power that made her knees weak.

"I want to understand," she replied, her voice barely above a whisper. "What is happening to our town? Who are you?"

The stranger studied her for a moment, then nodded. "You seek the truth. Very well. But know this: the path you are on is fraught with danger. The trials ahead will test not only your faith but your very soul."

He gestured to the altar, where a glowing symbol had appeared, pulsing with a rhythmic light. "This is the mark of the Almighty. It is a sign of the power that watches over you. But it is also a warning. The unseen hand of the divine moves in mysterious ways. Those who seek to understand must be prepared for the consequences."

Emily felt a surge of determination. "I am ready," she said, though fear still gripped her heart.

The stranger nodded again. "Then follow me. Together, we will uncover the truth and face the trials that lie ahead. But remember: not all who seek the light will find it. Some will be consumed by the darkness."

With that, he turned and began to walk back towards the town, the storm still raging above. Emily followed, her mind a whirlwind of thoughts and emotions. She knew that her life, and the lives of everyone in Havenbrook, were about to change in ways they could never have imagined.

The unseen hand of the Almighty was at work, and its whispers were growing louder. The true test of faith and resolve was only beginning.

4

The Chosen Ones

As dawn broke over Havenbrook, the town was still reeling from the night's tempest. The storm had left behind a trail of destruction: fallen trees, damaged homes, and a pervasive sense of unease. The stranger's ominous presence and the supernatural events that followed his arrival were the talk of the town. But amidst the chaos, a new mystery was unfolding—one that would test the resolve and faith of the townspeople in ways they could never have anticipated.

It began with a dream. Reverend Jameson awoke in a cold sweat, his heart pounding. In his dream, he had seen a series of symbols, glowing with an ethereal light, and heard a voice calling out to him—a voice that seemed to echo from the very heavens. The words were cryptic, but their message was clear: certain individuals in Havenbrook had been chosen for a divine purpose. They were to be guided by the Almighty through the trials to come.

He rose from his bed, still shaken by the vividness of the dream, and made his way to the study where Father Benedict was already poring over the ancient scrolls. The elderly monk looked up as Jameson entered, his eyes filled with a mixture of curiosity and concern.

"Another dream?" Benedict asked, his voice soft yet knowing.

Jameson nodded. "Yes. This one was different. It spoke of individuals in our town—people who have been chosen. We must find them."

Benedict leaned back in his chair, his expression thoughtful. "The scrolls mentioned such individuals—those marked by the divine. It seems your dream is another piece of the puzzle. We must act quickly."

Together, they devised a plan to identify the chosen ones. Jameson would speak to the congregation during Sunday service, urging anyone who had experienced strange visions or dreams to come forward. Meanwhile, Father Benedict would continue his work on deciphering the scrolls, searching for clues that might reveal the identities of these individuals.

The church was filled to capacity that Sunday, the pews packed with anxious faces. As Jameson stepped up to the pulpit, he felt the weight of his responsibility pressing down on him. He took a deep breath and began to speak, recounting his dream and the significance of the chosen ones. The congregation listened in stunned silence, their disbelief slowly giving way to a palpable tension.

After the service, a small group of townspeople approached Jameson, their expressions a mix of fear and hope. Among them was Emily, the young woman who had followed the stranger into the forest. She stepped forward, her eyes wide with determination.

"I've had dreams too," she confessed. "And I saw something... something that I can't explain."

Jameson nodded, recognizing the determination in her gaze. "You are not alone, Emily. We will face this together."

Others began to share their experiences: a farmer who had seen visions of angels in his fields, a schoolteacher who had heard voices in her sleep, and a young boy who had felt an inexplicable compulsion to draw symbols he couldn't understand. Each story added to the growing sense of wonder and dread.

That evening, the chosen ones gathered in the church, their faces illuminated by the flickering candlelight. Reverend Jameson and Father Benedict stood before them, a sense of solemn purpose uniting them all.

"The Almighty has chosen you for a reason," Jameson said, his voice steady. "We must prepare for the trials ahead. Together, we will find the strength to endure."

As the group began their preparations, the stranger watched from the shadows, his eyes glinting with an unreadable expression. He had expected resistance, disbelief, but instead, he found resolve. The people of Havenbrook were stronger than he had anticipated.

Days turned into weeks, and the chosen ones trained under the guidance of Jameson and Benedict. They learned to interpret the symbols and visions, to harness the strength of their faith, and to support one another in times of doubt. Emily emerged as a natural leader, her courage and determination inspiring those around her.

One evening, as the group gathered in the church to discuss their progress, the stranger appeared at the door. Silence fell over the room as he stepped inside, his presence commanding attention.

"You have done well," he said, his voice carrying a note of approval. "But the true test is yet to come."

Emily stood up, her eyes meeting his. "What do you mean?"

The stranger's gaze swept over the group, his expression grave. "The trials you have faced so far are but a prelude. The real challenge lies ahead. You must be ready to face the darkness, to confront the unknown. Only then will you prove yourselves worthy."

The room was thick with tension as his words sank in. The chosen ones exchanged glances, their resolve hardening. They knew they had come too far to turn back now.

That night, as they dispersed to their homes, each of them felt the weight of the stranger's words. Emily lay awake, staring at the ceiling as the events of the past weeks played through her mind. She knew that the coming trials would test them in ways they couldn't imagine, but she also knew that they were not alone. They had each other, and they had their faith.

As the clock struck midnight, a new vision came to her—clearer and more urgent than any before. She saw a figure standing at the edge of the forest, bathed in a halo of light. The figure beckoned to her, and she felt a surge of determination.

The chosen ones would face whatever lay ahead. They would unravel the mystery of the divine whispers, confront the darkness, and emerge stronger for it. The path was fraught with danger, but it was also illuminated by the light of faith.

And so, the stage was set for the ultimate test. The unseen hand of the Almighty was at work, guiding them through the shadows. The chosen ones were ready, their hearts filled with a resolve that burned brighter than the darkest night.

5

The Sacred Seal

The evening air was thick with anticipation as Emily made her way to the church, her mind racing with thoughts of the latest vision. The figure bathed in light had shown her a place deep in the forest, a location she instinctively knew held the key to understanding the trials that lay ahead. The urgency of the vision left her no choice but to act quickly.

Inside the church, Reverend Jameson and Father Benedict were deep in discussion. They had been tirelessly working to interpret the scrolls, but progress was slow, and frustration was mounting. The room was dimly lit by flickering candles, casting long shadows on the ancient stone walls.

Emily burst through the door, her face flushed with excitement. "I had another vision," she announced breathlessly. "I know where we need to go."

Jameson and Benedict looked up, their expressions a mix of curiosity and concern. "Tell us," Jameson urged, sensing the urgency in her voice.

Emily recounted her vision, describing the figure and the location in the forest. As she spoke, a sense of purpose filled the room. The chosen ones had been waiting for a sign, and it seemed they had finally received it.

"We must go there tonight," Emily insisted. "There's no time to waste."

Jameson nodded, his resolve firm. "Gather the others. We leave immediately."

The chosen ones assembled quickly, their faces determined despite the fear that lurked in their hearts. Armed with lanterns and a few supplies, they set out into the night, the forest looming ahead like a dark, impenetrable wall.

The journey was arduous, the path winding and overgrown. The forest was eerily silent, the only sounds their footsteps crunching on fallen leaves and the occasional hoot of an owl. Emily led the way, guided by an unseen force that seemed to pull her towards their destination.

As they delved deeper into the woods, the atmosphere grew heavier, charged with a palpable sense of foreboding. The trees seemed to close in around them, their twisted branches forming a labyrinth of shadows. The group moved in a tight formation, their lanterns casting small pools of light that barely penetrated the darkness.

After what felt like hours, they arrived at a clearing. In the center stood a large stone altar, covered in moss and vines, its surface inscribed with ancient symbols. Emily's breath caught in her throat as she recognized the scene from her vision. This was the place.

Reverend Jameson stepped forward, his lantern illuminating the altar. "This is it," he said softly, his voice tinged with awe. "The Sacred Seal."

The group gathered around the altar, their eyes wide with wonder and trepidation. Father Benedict began to examine the symbols, his fingers tracing the intricate patterns. "These markings," he murmured, "they're similar to those on the scrolls. This altar holds great significance."

As they studied the altar, the air around them grew colder, and a faint, otherworldly glow began to emanate from the stone. The chosen ones exchanged nervous glances, unsure of what was happening.

Suddenly, the ground beneath them trembled, and a deep rumbling echoed through the forest. The glow from the altar intensified, and a blinding light burst forth, enveloping the clearing. The group shielded their eyes, their hearts pounding with fear and anticipation.

When the light finally subsided, they found themselves standing before a newly revealed chamber, hidden beneath the altar. The entrance was marked by a large, intricately carved seal, its surface shimmering with a golden light.

Emily felt a surge of excitement and dread. "This is it," she whispered. "We've found the Sacred Seal."

Reverend Jameson stepped forward, his hand trembling as he reached out to touch the seal. The moment his fingers made contact, a low hum resonated through the air, and the seal began to pulse with a rhythmic glow.

"Stand back," Father Benedict warned, his voice urgent. "Something's happening."

The chosen ones retreated, watching in awe as the seal slowly lifted, revealing a hidden staircase descending into the earth. A sense of both wonder and fear gripped them as they peered into the darkness below.

"We must go down," Emily said, her voice steady despite the fear gnawing at her insides. "This is what we've been preparing for."

With a deep breath, she led the way, descending the narrow staircase into the unknown. The others followed, their lanterns casting eerie shadows on the stone walls. The air grew colder the deeper they went, and an oppressive silence filled the space, broken only by their footsteps echoing off the walls.

The staircase ended in a large underground chamber, its walls adorned with more of the ancient symbols. In the center of the room stood a pedestal, upon which rested a large, ornate book bound in leather and gold. The book seemed to radiate a faint, otherworldly light.

Father Benedict approached the pedestal, his eyes wide with reverence. "This is the Book of Prophecies," he said, his voice trembling with awe. "The key to understanding the trials and the Sacred Seal."

Reverend Jameson stepped forward, his hand reaching out to touch the book. The moment his fingers brushed the cover, a surge of energy coursed through him, and the book sprang open, its pages flipping rapidly before settling on a particular passage.

The group gathered around, peering at the ancient text. The symbols seemed to come alive, glowing with an ethereal light. As they read the passage, the full weight of their mission became clear. The trials were not merely tests of faith but challenges that would require every ounce of their courage, wisdom, and strength.

Suddenly, a voice echoed through the chamber, low and resonant. "You have found the Sacred Seal and the Book of Prophecies. The trials ahead will test your very souls. Only those with unwavering faith and unbreakable bonds will prevail."

The chosen ones exchanged determined glances, their resolve solidifying. They knew the path ahead would be fraught with danger, but they were ready to face whatever challenges the Almighty had in store for them.

As they left the chamber and ascended the staircase, the air seemed to hum with a newfound energy. The Sacred Seal had been revealed, and with it, the next step in their journey. The chosen ones were prepared to confront the darkness and uncover the truth behind the divine whispers that had led them to this moment.

The forest seemed less foreboding as they made their way back to Havenbrook, their hearts filled with a renewed sense of purpose. The trials ahead would be daunting, but they had faith in each other and in the divine guidance that had brought them this far.

Little did they know, the true test of their faith and resolve was just beginning.

6

The Prophet's Dilemma

The revelation of the Sacred Seal and the discovery of the Book of Prophecies had left the chosen ones both exhilarated and anxious. They now possessed a guide to the trials that lay ahead, but the weight of their mission bore heavily on their shoulders. As the days passed, the anticipation of the unknown grew, and with it, a sense of unease that permeated the town of Havenbrook.

Reverend Jameson spent long hours in the church, studying the ancient text and seeking divine guidance. The symbols and passages were complex, filled with layers of meaning that required careful interpretation. Father Benedict assisted him, his vast knowledge of ancient languages proving invaluable. Together, they worked tirelessly, deciphering the messages and preparing for the trials.

One evening, as the sun set and cast long shadows across the church, a stranger arrived at the door. He was a tall man with piercing blue eyes and a presence that commanded attention. His arrival was unexpected, and the townsfolk quickly gathered, curious and wary.

Reverend Jameson stepped forward, his heart pounding with a mixture of hope and fear. "Welcome to Havenbrook," he said, his voice steady. "How may we help you?"

The stranger smiled, his gaze steady. "I have come with a message," he announced, his voice resonating with an otherworldly authority. "I am a prophet, sent to guide you through the trials that await."

A murmur of disbelief rippled through the crowd. Jameson exchanged a glance with Father Benedict, both men sensing the gravity of the situation. They invited the prophet into the church, where he began to share his vision.

"The trials you face are but the beginning," the prophet declared, his voice echoing in the dimly lit room. "The Almighty has chosen you for a purpose, and it is my duty to lead you. You must follow my guidance without question if you are to succeed."

Jameson felt a knot of tension in his chest. While the prophet's words were compelling, he couldn't shake the feeling of unease. He had spent countless hours with the Book of Prophecies, and something about the prophet's demeanor and demands didn't sit right with him.

As the days passed, the prophet integrated himself into the lives of the chosen ones. He offered guidance, interpreting the prophecies with an authority that left little room for doubt. Yet, beneath his calm exterior, there was a growing sense of urgency, as if time itself were running out.

Emily, ever observant, noticed the subtle changes in the prophet's behavior. His initial warmth had given way to a sternness that bordered on severity. His instructions became more demanding, and any deviation from his guidance was met with disapproval. She confided her concerns to Jameson, who shared her unease.

One night, Emily decided to follow the prophet. She moved silently through the darkened streets of Havenbrook, her heart pounding with a mixture of fear and determination. She shadowed him to the edge of the forest, where he disappeared into the trees.

Emily's curiosity drove her forward, and she soon found herself in a secluded glade. There, the prophet stood before an ancient stone altar, similar to the one they had discovered beneath the Sacred Seal. He was speaking in a language she didn't understand, his voice low and urgent.

She watched in stunned silence as a shadowy figure emerged from the darkness, its presence sending a chill down her spine. The figure handed the prophet a small, glowing orb, which he accepted with reverence.

Emily's breath caught in her throat. She knew she had stumbled upon something significant, something that could change the course of their mission. She turned and fled back to the town, her mind racing with the implications of what she had seen.

The next morning, she sought out Jameson and Father Benedict, recounting her experience in hushed tones. They listened intently, their expressions growing graver with each word. It was clear that the prophet was not what he seemed.

"We must confront him," Jameson said, his voice firm. "But we must be cautious. If he truly is a false prophet, we need evidence to convince the others."

That night, under the cover of darkness, the three of them made their way to the glade. They hid among the trees, watching as the prophet once again performed his secret ritual. The shadowy figure appeared, and this time, they were prepared.

Jameson stepped forward, his lantern casting a circle of light. "Stop!" he commanded, his voice ringing through the glade. "We know what you're doing."

The prophet turned, his eyes flashing with anger. "You do not understand," he said, his voice filled with a cold menace. "I am your only hope. Without me, you will fail."

Benedict stepped forward, holding up a passage from the Book of Prophecies. "You twist the words of the Almighty for your gain," he said. "We have seen the truth."

The shadowy figure retreated into the darkness, and the prophet's demeanor changed. He laughed, a sound devoid of warmth. "You are fools," he sneered. "You think you can defy me? The trials are already upon you, and you are unprepared."

With a sudden movement, he hurled the glowing orb to the ground. A blinding light filled the glade, and when it faded, the prophet was gone. The chosen ones were left standing in stunned silence, the weight of their situation settling heavily on their shoulders.

They returned to Havenbrook, knowing that the true trials were only beginning. The prophet's betrayal had shaken their faith, but it had also steeled their resolve. They were determined to face whatever lay ahead, united in their quest for truth and guided by the whispers of the Almighty.

7

The Divine Conspiracy

The morning after the prophet's disappearance, Havenbrook awoke to a palpable tension in the air. The chosen ones, though relieved to be rid of the false prophet, felt an unease that gnawed at their hearts. They gathered in the church, their faces etched with worry as they discussed the implications of the prophet's deception.

"We've been misled," Father Benedict said gravely, pacing before the altar. "But we cannot let this shake our faith. We must continue our mission and remain vigilant."

Reverend Jameson nodded in agreement. "We need to decipher the remaining prophecies and uncover the true path the Almighty has set for us."

Emily, who had been quiet throughout the discussion, suddenly spoke up. "There's something else. The shadowy figure I saw with the prophet—it felt like more than just an accomplice. It felt... powerful, otherworldly."

Her words hung in the air, sending a shiver down the spines of the gathered group. They realized that their struggle was not merely against human deception, but against forces far greater and more sinister than they had imagined.

Determined to uncover the truth, the chosen ones intensified their efforts to decode the ancient scrolls. Days turned into nights, and the boundaries between them blurred as they poured over the texts. Each passage revealed more about the trials to come, but also hinted at a deeper conspiracy that entwined the fate of Havenbrook with that of the world.

One evening, as the group labored in the dim candlelight, Reverend Jameson stumbled upon a passage that sent chills down his spine. It spoke of a hidden order, a clandestine group that sought to manipulate divine prophecies for their own gain. This order had existed for centuries, its members working from the shadows to influence events and control the destiny of mankind.

"They call themselves the Divine Council," Jameson read aloud, his voice trembling. "Their goal is to harness the power of the Almighty for their own purposes, and they will stop at nothing to achieve it."

The room fell silent as the gravity of the revelation sank in. The false prophet had been a pawn of this sinister group, and the chosen ones now found themselves in the crosshairs of a dangerous conspiracy.

Emily clenched her fists, her resolve hardening. "We have to expose them," she said fiercely. "We have to show the world the truth."

Father Benedict nodded. "But we must be careful. They are powerful and will not hesitate to silence those who stand in their way."

As they continued their work, strange events began to unfold in Havenbrook. People reported seeing shadowy figures lurking in the alleys and hearing whispers in the dead of night. A sense of paranoia and fear spread through the town, making it clear that the Divine Council was aware of the chosen ones' efforts and was watching them closely.

One night, as Emily walked home from the church, she felt a presence following her. She quickened her pace, her heart pounding in her chest. The footsteps behind her grew louder, and she could hear the rustle of leaves and the faint whisper of voices. Panic surged through her, but she forced herself to remain calm.

Turning a corner, she ducked into a narrow alley and pressed herself against the wall, her breath coming in ragged gasps. The footsteps passed by, and she dared to peek out, catching a glimpse of a hooded figure disappearing into the shadows.

Emily knew she had to warn the others. She ran to Jameson's house, her fear giving her speed. She banged on the door, her urgency evident.

Jameson opened the door, his eyes widening in concern. "Emily, what is it?"

"They're here," she gasped. "The Divine Council. They're watching us."

Jameson's face hardened. "We need to regroup. Gather everyone at the church. We'll be safer together."

Within the hour, the chosen ones were assembled in the church, their fear mingling with determination. They barricaded the doors and windows, creating a makeshift fortress against the unseen threat that loomed over them.

As they huddled together, Father Benedict addressed the group. "We must stay strong. The Divine Council thrives on fear and secrecy. If we expose them, their power will diminish."

Reverend Jameson nodded. "We need a plan. We have to gather evidence of their existence and their plans. And we need allies—people outside

Havenbrook who can help us spread the truth."

Emily stepped forward, her eyes blazing with determination. "I'll go to the city. I have a friend there who's a journalist. She can help us get the word out."

The group agreed, and preparations were made for Emily's journey. She left under the cover of darkness, determined to find help and expose the Divine Council's machinations.

Back in Havenbrook, the chosen ones continued their efforts, even as the sense of danger grew. They worked in shifts, keeping watch and decoding the scrolls, knowing that time was running out. The tension was palpable, each creak of the old church's timbers causing their hearts to race.

Days passed without word from Emily, and the chosen ones began to fear the worst. Just as their hope was starting to wane, a letter arrived, smuggled into the church by a sympathetic townsfolk. It was from Emily, and her message was both a relief and a call to action.

She had reached the city safely and made contact with her journalist friend. They were working to uncover more about the Divine Council and gather evidence that could expose their conspiracy. But Emily also warned that the Council was tightening its grip, and the chosen ones needed to be prepared for an imminent confrontation.

As the sun set over Havenbrook, casting long shadows over the church, the chosen ones steeled themselves for the battle ahead. The Divine Council's influence was vast, but their faith and determination were stronger. They knew that the true power lay in the truth and in their unwavering belief in the divine guidance that had brought them together.

The stage was set for the ultimate confrontation. The whispers of the Almighty had led them to this moment, and the chosen ones were ready to face the darkness, uncover the conspiracy, and reveal the light of truth to the world.

8

The Last Covenant

The chill of the early morning air nipped at Emily's cheeks as she returned to Havenbrook, her heart heavy with the weight of the information she carried. The journey back had been fraught with danger; every shadow seemed to hide an enemy, every sound a potential threat. But now, as she approached the town, a sense of urgency propelled her forward. The chosen ones needed to know what she had discovered about the Divine Council and the last covenant that could change their fate.

Reverend Jameson and Father Benedict were waiting at the church, their faces etched with concern. Emily entered the sanctuary, her eyes scanning the room to ensure they were alone. She closed the door behind her and locked it, her hands trembling.

"I've learned something," she said, her voice barely above a whisper. "The Divine Council is planning a ritual. It's called the Last Covenant. If they succeed, they will gain unimaginable power."

Jameson frowned, his mind racing. "What kind of ritual?"

Emily took a deep breath, trying to steady her nerves. "The Last Covenant is a binding ritual. It requires a sacrifice—someone of pure faith. The ritual will merge their power with that of the Council, giving them control over the prophecies and, potentially, over the divine itself."

A heavy silence fell over the room as the gravity of her words sank in. Father Benedict's face paled, and Jameson's expression hardened with resolve.

"We can't let that happen," Jameson said, his voice firm. "We need to find out where and when this ritual is taking place and stop it."

Emily nodded. "I have a lead. There's a place in the forest, deeper than we've ever gone. It's a hidden temple, ancient and powerful. That's where they plan to perform the ritual."

They quickly formulated a plan. The chosen ones would venture into the forest that night, under the cover of darkness, to locate the temple and disrupt the ritual. It was a perilous mission, but there was no alternative. Failure was not an option.

As night fell, the chosen ones gathered their supplies and prepared for the journey. They moved silently through the town, their footsteps muffled by the thick carpet of leaves that covered the ground. The forest loomed ahead, a dark, impenetrable wall of shadows and secrets.

Emily led the way, her senses heightened by the knowledge of what lay ahead. The deeper they went, the thicker the trees became, their twisted branches forming a canopy that blocked out the moonlight. The air grew colder, and an eerie silence settled over the group, broken only by the occasional rustle of leaves or snap of a twig.

After what felt like hours, they reached the clearing Emily had described. The hidden temple stood before them, its stone walls covered in ancient symbols that seemed to pulse with a faint, otherworldly light. The entrance was guarded by two statues, their features worn by time but still exuding an aura of power and menace.

The chosen ones exchanged nervous glances, their resolve tested by the sight of the temple. Jameson stepped forward, his lantern casting a weak light on the stone steps.

"Stay close," he whispered. "And be ready for anything."

They entered the temple, their footsteps echoing in the cavernous space. The air inside was thick with the scent of incense and ancient dust. They moved cautiously, their lanterns illuminating the intricate carvings on the walls—scenes of rituals and sacrifices, of gods and men intertwined in a dance of power and submission.

As they ventured deeper into the temple, they heard voices—low, chanting voices that sent shivers down their spines. They followed the sound, their hearts pounding with fear and anticipation.

They emerged into a large chamber, its center dominated by a stone altar. Around it stood the members of the Divine Council, their faces obscured by hooded robes. The air was charged with energy, the chanting growing louder and more intense.

On the altar lay a young woman, her eyes wide with fear. She was bound by thick ropes, her wrists and ankles secured to the stone. Emily recognized her as one of the townsfolk, a girl known for her unwavering faith and kindness.

"We have to stop them," Emily whispered, her voice trembling with urgency.

Jameson nodded, his eyes locked on the scene before them. "Follow my lead."

They moved swiftly, spreading out to surround the chamber. Jameson stepped forward, his voice ringing out with authority. "Stop this madness!"

The chanting ceased, and the members of the Divine Council turned to face them. The leader, a tall figure with piercing eyes, stepped forward, a sneer on his lips.

"You are too late," he said, his voice dripping with contempt. "The ritual has begun. The Last Covenant will be fulfilled."

Jameson raised his lantern, its light casting long shadows on the walls. "We will not let you corrupt the will of the Almighty. Release her, or face the consequences."

The leader laughed, a cold, mirthless sound. "You are fools. You think you can defy us? The power of the divine will be ours."

Emily felt a surge of fear and determination. She knew they had to act quickly. She signaled to the others, and they sprang into action, rushing towards the altar.

The chamber erupted into chaos. The chosen ones clashed with the members of the Divine Council, their lanterns casting frantic beams of light as they fought. Emily reached the altar and began to untie the girl, her hands shaking with urgency.

The leader of the Council shouted an incantation, and the air crackled with energy. A blinding light filled the chamber, and Emily felt herself being thrown back by an invisible force. She landed hard on the stone floor, her vision blurred by the intensity of the light.

As the light faded, she saw Jameson standing before the altar, his face grim with determination. He held the Book of Prophecies in his hands, its pages glowing with an ethereal light.

"The Almighty's will cannot be corrupted," he declared, his voice resonating with power. "Your ritual ends now."

The leader of the Council screamed in rage, but it was too late. The Book of Prophecies glowed brighter, its light enveloping the chamber. The members of the Council were thrown back, their robes burning away to reveal their true, twisted forms.

With a final, deafening roar, the chamber was plunged into darkness. The chosen ones lay on the stone floor, their bodies aching from the battle. Slowly, they rose, their eyes adjusting to the dim light of their lanterns.

Emily rushed to the altar, her heart pounding with fear. The girl was still there, her eyes wide with shock but unharmed. Emily untied her, tears of relief streaming down her face.

"We did it," she whispered, her voice filled with a mixture of disbelief and triumph. "We stopped them."

Jameson and the others gathered around, their faces reflecting the same mix of emotions. They had faced the darkness and emerged victorious, but they knew their journey was far from over.

The Last Covenant had been thwarted, but the whispers of the Almighty continued to guide them. The trials ahead would be no less daunting, but the chosen ones were ready to face them, united in their faith and determination.

9

The Whispering Shadows

The chosen ones returned to Havenbrook in the dead of night, the eerie stillness of the town starkly contrasting with the chaos they had left behind in the temple. The weight of their victory against the Divine Council hung heavily upon them, but a new sense of dread began to seep into their hearts. The shadows seemed to grow longer, and the whispers they had fought to silence echoed even louder in their minds.

Emily and Reverend Jameson stayed behind in the church, their faces lined with exhaustion and concern. The young woman they had saved rested on a pew, her breaths shallow and her eyes wide with fear. The night's events had left her shaken, and she clung to Emily for comfort.

"We must protect her," Jameson said, his voice low but resolute. "The Council will not give up so easily. They'll come for her again."

Emily nodded, her gaze fixed on the girl. "We need to keep her safe. And we need to find out more about the whispers. They're growing stronger."

Jameson agreed, but before they could plan further, a sudden chill filled the church. The candles flickered, and an unnatural darkness crept into the corners of the room. The whispers grew louder, an insidious murmur that seemed to seep into their very souls.

Emily stood, her heart pounding. "Do you hear that?" she asked, her voice barely above a whisper.

Jameson nodded, his expression grim. "The shadows... they're alive."

The two moved cautiously through the church, their lanterns casting weak beams of light that seemed to be swallowed by the encroaching darkness. The whispers grew louder, more distinct, as if they were surrounded by unseen entities.

"Beware the darkness," the whispers hissed. "Beware the shadows."

Emily felt a cold hand brush against her arm, and she jumped, nearly dropping her lantern. "What was that?" she gasped, her voice trembling.

Jameson held his lantern higher, illuminating the empty pews and the ancient stone walls. "We are not alone," he said. "The shadows are watching us."

Suddenly, the door to the church burst open, and Father Benedict rushed in, his face pale and his eyes wide with fear. "They're here!" he shouted. "The shadows have come alive!"

Before they could react, the darkness surged forward, enveloping the room in a suffocating shroud. The whispers became a cacophony, a chorus of malevolent voices that seemed to come from all directions.

"Run!" Jameson shouted, grabbing Emily's hand and pulling her towards the back of the church. Father Benedict followed, his steps faltering as the shadows clung to him, trying to drag him down.

They burst through a side door and into the night, the cold air biting at their skin. The darkness seemed to follow them, a living entity that pursued them through the deserted streets of Havenbrook.

"We need to find the others!" Emily shouted, her voice barely audible over the roar of the shadows. "We can't fight this alone!"

Jameson led them towards the center of town, where the rest of the chosen ones were likely hiding. They moved quickly, their lanterns flickering as the shadows pressed in around them. The whispers continued, now filled with mocking laughter and threats.

"You cannot escape us," they hissed. "The darkness is eternal."

As they reached the town square, they saw the others huddled together, their faces pale with fear. The shadows had surrounded them, a swirling mass of darkness that seemed impenetrable.

Jameson raised his lantern high, the light casting a weak glow that barely penetrated the darkness. "We have to stand together," he shouted. "The light will protect us!"

The chosen ones gathered around, their lanterns held high. The combined light pushed back the shadows, creating a small circle of safety in the midst of the darkness.

"We need to find the source," Emily said, her voice filled with determination. "There has to be something driving these shadows, something we can stop."

Father Benedict nodded. "The whispers... they spoke of a place. An ancient well, hidden in the forest. It's said to be a gateway to the underworld, a place where the darkness dwells."

Jameson's eyes widened. "The Well of Shadows," he said. "It's mentioned in the prophecies. If we can close it, we might be able to stop the shadows."

With no time to lose, the chosen ones set off towards the forest, the shadows nipping at their heels. They moved quickly, their lanterns lighting the way as they navigated the twisted paths and dense underbrush.

The whispers grew louder as they approached the well, a low, insidious chant that seemed to vibrate through the air. The forest itself seemed to come alive, the trees twisting and writhing as if possessed by the same dark force.

At last, they reached a clearing, where an ancient stone well stood. The air around it was thick with darkness, a swirling vortex of shadows that seemed to pulse with a malevolent energy.

"We have to seal it," Jameson said, his voice trembling. "We need to use the Book of Prophecies."

Father Benedict stepped forward, holding the book aloft. "The power of the Almighty will guide us," he said, his voice filled with conviction.

As he began to chant the ancient incantation, the shadows surged forward, their whispers becoming a deafening roar. The chosen ones formed a circle around the well, their lanterns casting a protective light that kept the darkness at bay.

The ground trembled, and a blinding light burst forth from the well, illuminating the forest with an otherworldly glow. The shadows recoiled, their whispers turning to screams as the light grew stronger.

With a final, powerful chant, Father Benedict thrust the book into the well. The light intensified, and the shadows were drawn into the vortex, their forms disintegrating as they were consumed by the divine power.

The forest fell silent, the whispers finally silenced. The chosen ones stood in stunned silence, their hearts pounding with relief and exhaustion. The well was sealed, and the darkness had been vanquished.

As they made their way back to Havenbrook, the first rays of dawn broke through the trees, casting a warm, golden light on the town. The whispers were gone, and the shadows had been driven back. But the chosen ones knew that their journey was far from over. The trials ahead would be no less daunting, but they were ready to face them, united in their faith and determination.

The light of the Almighty had guided them through the darkness, and they would continue to follow its path, no matter where it led.

10

The Judgment

The first light of dawn cast long shadows over Havenbrook as the chosen ones returned from their final confrontation. Exhaustion weighed heavily on their shoulders, but a newfound sense of peace and unity buoyed their spirits. The Divine Council's power had been shattered, and the whispers of the Almighty had led them to a decisive victory. Yet, an unspoken understanding lingered among them—they were not yet free from the trials of their journey.

Reverend Jameson and Emily stood at the church's entrance, watching the sun rise over the horizon. The golden light bathed the town in a warm glow, a stark contrast to the darkness they had faced. Father Benedict approached, his face lined with both relief and lingering concern.

"We've come so far," he said softly, "but I fear the final judgment is yet to come."

Emily nodded, her eyes scanning the peaceful town. "We need to prepare. The prophecies spoke of a reckoning, a test that would determine our fate."

Jameson turned to them, his expression resolute. "Gather everyone. We must face this together, as we always have."

By mid-morning, the chosen ones were assembled in the church, their faces reflecting a mixture of hope and apprehension. The air was thick with anticipation, as if the very walls of the ancient building were holding their breath.

Jameson stood before them, the Book of Prophecies in his hands. "We have faced many trials and emerged stronger for it," he began, his voice steady. "But the final judgment awaits. The Almighty will weigh our deeds and our hearts. We must be ready to face whatever comes."

As he spoke, a sudden chill swept through the room, extinguishing the candles and plunging them into darkness. The chosen ones gasped, their eyes straining to see in the dim light.

A low, resonant voice filled the air, echoing through the church. "You have come far, but the final test is upon you. Prepare yourselves for the judgment."

The voice seemed to come from everywhere and nowhere, its power palpable. The chosen ones exchanged nervous glances, their resolve tested by the unseen presence.

Suddenly, the ground beneath them trembled, and a blinding light filled the room. When the light subsided, they found themselves standing in a vast, ethereal landscape, unlike anything they had ever seen. The sky was a swirling tapestry of colors, and the ground was a shimmering expanse of light and shadow.

At the center of this otherworldly realm stood a figure, radiating an intense, divine energy. The figure's face was obscured by a brilliant halo, and its presence filled the chosen ones with a mixture of awe and fear.

"Welcome," the figure said, its voice resonating with an otherworldly power. "You stand before the Almighty for the final judgment."

Reverend Jameson stepped forward, his heart pounding in his chest. "We are ready to face the judgment," he said, his voice unwavering. "We have followed the path set before us and faced every trial with faith and unity."

The figure nodded, its halo pulsing with light. "You have indeed faced many trials, but the final test is one of the heart. Each of you must confront your deepest fears and darkest secrets. Only then can you truly be judged."

As the figure spoke, the landscape shifted and changed. Each of the chosen ones found themselves standing alone in a separate, isolated space, their surroundings reflecting their innermost fears.

Emily found herself in a dark, oppressive forest, the trees closing in around her. The whispers she had fought so hard to silence returned, louder and more insistent. She felt a presence behind her and turned to see a shadowy figure, its eyes glowing with malevolent intent.

"Do you think you can escape your past?" the figure hissed. "Do you think you are worthy of the Almighty's favor?"

Emily's heart raced, but she stood her ground. "I have faced my fears and my past," she said, her voice steady. "I am not perfect, but I have strived to do what is right."

The figure laughed, a cold, mocking sound. "We shall see," it said, before vanishing into the darkness.

Elsewhere, Jameson found himself standing before a vast, empty cathedral. The silence was deafening, and the weight of his responsibilities pressed down on him like a physical force. He heard a familiar voice and turned to see his late wife, her face filled with sadness.

"You have always put your duty before everything else," she said softly. "But what of your own heart? Have you truly lived, or have you merely existed?"

Jameson's eyes filled with tears. "I have tried to serve faithfully," he whispered. "But I have also made mistakes. I can only hope that my intentions were pure."

Father Benedict stood on a precipice, overlooking a churning sea of doubt and regret. He saw the faces of those he had failed, their accusations ringing in his ears. "You claim to be a man of faith, but where was your faith when it truly mattered?" they demanded.

Benedict clenched his fists, his heart aching with guilt. "I am flawed, as we all are," he said. "But I have never stopped striving to be better, to seek redemption."

As each of the chosen ones faced their personal trials, they realized that the judgment was not about perfection but about the journey, the struggle, and the growth they had experienced. One by one, they confronted their fears, confessed their sins, and affirmed their commitment to the path of light.

The ethereal landscape began to dissolve, and they found themselves back in the church, standing before the radiant figure. The figure's halo pulsed with a warm, golden light, and its voice was filled with a gentle power.

"You have faced the final test and revealed the truth of your hearts," the figure said. "The Almighty has seen your struggles, your failures, and your triumphs. You are not perfect, but you are worthy."

The chosen ones felt a wave of relief and gratitude wash over them. They had been judged not by their perfection but by their faith, their unity, and their willingness to confront their deepest fears.

The figure's light grew brighter, filling the church with a divine radiance. "Go forth with the knowledge that you are guided by the light of the Almighty. Your journey is not over, but you have proven your worth."

As the light faded, the chosen ones found themselves alone in the church once more, the dawn's light streaming through the stained glass windows. They looked at each other, their hearts filled with a renewed sense of purpose and unity.

They had faced the final judgment and emerged stronger for it. The path ahead would still be fraught with challenges, but they knew that they were not alone. The whispers of the Almighty would continue to guide them, and together, they would face whatever the future held, united in their faith and their commitment to the light.

11

The Veil of Deception

The dawn had barely broken when Emily awoke with a start, a cold sweat clinging to her skin. The judgment they had faced still echoed in her mind, but the clarity and peace that had come with it seemed to be slipping away. She glanced around the small room, its shadows stretching eerily in the first light of day. Something felt wrong, deeply wrong.

She dressed quickly and hurried to the church, her heart pounding with a sense of impending doom. As she pushed open the heavy doors, she found Reverend Jameson and Father Benedict already there, their faces grave and eyes shadowed with worry.

"Did you feel it?" she asked breathlessly. "Something's not right."

Jameson nodded, his expression tense. "I felt it too. As if the peace we earned is being threatened."

Father Benedict leaned over the Book of Prophecies, his fingers tracing the ancient symbols. "The final judgment may not have been the end. There could be another trial, one hidden from us until now."

As they pored over the scrolls, a low, ominous hum filled the church. The candles flickered, casting unsettling shadows on the walls. The air grew thick with a sense of foreboding, and the whispers that had plagued them before seemed to return, louder and more insistent.

Emily's heart raced. "The whispers... they're back. But how? We destroyed the source."

Jameson's face hardened with determination. "We need to find out what's causing this. The Divine Council may have a hidden ace, something we missed."

Suddenly, the door burst open, and one of the chosen ones, a young man named Daniel, stumbled in, his face pale with fear. "You need to come quickly," he gasped. "The town... it's changing."

They followed Daniel through the streets of Havenbrook, their dread mounting with every step. The once familiar town seemed twisted and distorted, as if a dark veil had been cast over it. Buildings appeared older, more decrepit, and shadows seemed to move with a life of their own.

As they reached the town square, they saw a group of townsfolk gathered around a central figure, their faces blank and eyes glazed. The figure was cloaked in darkness, its features obscured by a hood. The whispers grew louder, more insidious, as the figure raised its head, revealing piercing eyes that seemed to see into their very souls.

"You thought you had won," the figure hissed, its voice a chilling echo. "But the final test is yet to come. The veil of deception has been cast, and only the truth can break it."

Emily felt a cold dread settle in her chest. "Who are you?" she demanded, her voice trembling with a mixture of fear and defiance.

The figure laughed, a sound devoid of warmth. "I am the Harbinger, the one who brings forth the final deception. The Divine Council may be defeated, but their legacy lives on. You must face the ultimate trial, or your town will be lost to the darkness forever."

Jameson stepped forward, his face a mask of resolve. "We will not be deceived. We will uncover the truth and banish this darkness."

The Harbinger's eyes glinted with malice. "Very well. But know this: the veil is strong, and the truth is buried deep. You must confront your deepest fears and unravel the lies that bind you."

With a final, mocking laugh, the Harbinger vanished, leaving the chosen ones standing in the distorted town square. The townsfolk began to disperse, their faces still blank, as if they were sleepwalking.

"We need to act quickly," Jameson said, his voice urgent. "The longer the veil remains, the stronger it will become. We must find the source and destroy it."

Father Benedict nodded. "The Book of Prophecies may hold the key. There are passages we haven't fully deciphered, clues that could lead us to the truth."

As they returned to the church, the whispers followed them, growing louder and more menacing. The atmosphere was thick with tension, and the shadows seemed to close in around them.

They worked tirelessly, decoding the ancient texts and searching for answers. The Book of Prophecies revealed a hidden passage, one that spoke of a place where the veil was weakest, where the truth could be uncovered.

"It's the old mill," Emily said, her eyes wide with realization. "That's where we need to go."

The chosen ones gathered their supplies and set out for the old mill, their hearts heavy with anticipation. The journey was fraught with danger, the whispers growing louder with every step, urging them to turn back, to give in to the darkness.

As they reached the mill, they found it shrouded in an unnatural darkness, the air thick with a sense of malevolence. The whispers became a cacophony, their insidious words clawing at their minds.

"We must stay strong," Jameson said, his voice steady. "Remember our faith and our unity. That is our strength."

They entered the mill, their lanterns casting weak beams of light that barely penetrated the darkness. The air was cold and damp, and the walls seemed to close in around them.

At the center of the mill, they found a large, ornate mirror, its surface covered in a thick layer of dust. The mirror seemed to pulse with a dark energy, the source of the veil of deception.

Emily stepped forward, her heart pounding. "This is it. We need to destroy it."

As she reached out to touch the mirror, a blinding light filled the room, and the Harbinger's voice echoed through the air. "You cannot escape the truth. You must face it."

The light intensified, and the chosen ones found themselves in a twisted reflection of the town, a dark and distorted version of Havenbrook. The townsfolk were there, their faces twisted with fear and despair, their eyes filled with a hollow emptiness.

"You must confront the lies that bind you," the Harbinger's voice echoed.

"Only then can you break the veil."

The chosen ones moved through the twisted town, facing their deepest fears and unraveling the lies that had been woven into their lives. They confronted their past mistakes, their hidden guilt, and their unspoken regrets, each revelation bringing them closer to the truth.

As they faced their fears, the twisted town began to dissolve, the darkness lifting and the whispers fading. The mirror's surface cracked, and the dark energy that had held it together dissipated.

With a final, resounding shatter, the mirror broke, and the chosen ones found themselves back in the old mill, the veil of deception lifted. The air was clear, and the oppressive darkness was gone.

They stood together, their hearts filled with a sense of relief and triumph. They had faced the ultimate deception and emerged victorious, their faith and unity stronger than ever.

As they returned to the town, the first rays of dawn broke through the clouds, casting a warm, golden light over Havenbrook. The whispers were silenced, and the shadows banished.

The chosen ones knew that their journey was not over, but they were ready to face whatever challenges lay ahead. The light of the Almighty guided them, and together, they would continue to seek the truth and protect their town from the darkness.

12

The Eternal Echo

The dawn of a new day brought a fragile peace to Havenbrook. The chosen ones had lifted the veil of deception, but the air still felt charged with an undercurrent of unease. Emily, Reverend Jameson, and Father Benedict knew that despite their recent victory, something remained unresolved. The whispers had ceased, but the echoes of the past trials lingered in their minds.

In the early hours, a messenger arrived at the church, bearing an urgent letter. It was from an old acquaintance of Father Benedict, a historian named Professor Alden, who had been studying the same ancient texts and prophecies. The letter spoke of a final piece to the puzzle, an ancient relic known as the Eternal Echo, said to hold the power to either seal their victory or unleash an even greater darkness. The relic was believed to be hidden in the catacombs beneath the ruins of an old monastery on the outskirts of Havenbrook.

Father Benedict read the letter aloud, his voice filled with both hope and trepidation. "The Eternal Echo," he said, "is the key to ensuring that the darkness remains banished. But it is also a test, the final trial. We must retrieve it and determine its true nature."

Jameson nodded, his face set with determination. "We have come this far together. We will face this final trial as one."

The chosen ones prepared for their journey, gathering their supplies and steeling themselves for whatever lay ahead. The path to the ruins was fraught with uncertainty, but they moved with a sense of purpose, their faith guiding them through the dense forest and treacherous terrain.

As they approached the ruins, a sense of foreboding settled over them. The once-grand monastery was now a crumbling relic, its stone walls covered in moss and vines. The entrance to the catacombs lay hidden beneath a collapsed archway, and the air was thick with the scent of damp earth and decay.

Emily led the way, her lantern casting a weak glow on the narrow, winding staircase that descended into the darkness. The catacombs were a labyrinth of tunnels and chambers, their walls lined with the skeletal remains of long-forgotten monks. The silence was oppressive, broken only by the echo of their footsteps.

As they ventured deeper, they felt a growing sense of unease. The air grew colder, and an almost palpable energy seemed to hum through the stone walls. It was as if the catacombs themselves were alive, watching and waiting.

Finally, they reached a large, circular chamber. At its center stood a pedestal, upon which rested a small, ornate box. The box was intricately carved with ancient symbols, and it seemed to pulse with a faint, otherworldly light.

"This must be it," Emily whispered, her voice trembling with a mixture of awe and fear. "The Eternal Echo."

Reverend Jameson approached the pedestal, his hand reaching out to touch the box. As his fingers brushed the surface, a blinding light filled the chamber, and a deep, resonant voice echoed through the air.

"You have come seeking the Eternal Echo," the voice intoned. "But know this: its power is both a blessing and a curse. To wield it is to face the ultimate test of your faith and resolve."

The light intensified, and the chosen ones found themselves standing in a vast, ethereal landscape, much like the one they had encountered during the final judgment. The voice continued, its tone both commanding and compassionate.

"The Eternal Echo holds the power to seal the darkness or to release it anew. Each of you must confront the truth within your hearts and determine the fate of Havenbrook."

Emily felt a surge of fear and determination. She knew that this was the moment they had been preparing for, the culmination of their journey. She stepped forward, her voice steady despite the fear that gnawed at her insides.

"We are ready," she said. "We will face this trial together."

The voice responded with a sense of approval. "Then let the trial begin."

The landscape shifted, and each of the chosen ones found themselves alone, faced with a vision of their deepest fears and doubts. Emily stood in a desolate wasteland, the ground cracked and barren. She saw her friends and family, their faces twisted with pain and despair, accusing her of failing them.

"You think you can save them?" a voice whispered, dripping with malice. "You are nothing. You will only bring ruin."

Emily's heart ached, but she refused to be swayed. "I am not perfect," she said, her voice rising with conviction. "But I have always tried to do what is right. I will not be defeated by fear."

As she spoke, the wasteland began to dissolve, replaced by a warm, golden light. The accusing faces vanished, replaced by the supportive, encouraging gazes of her friends.

Reverend Jameson found himself in a grand, empty cathedral, the silence deafening. He saw himself standing at the pulpit, preaching to an empty congregation. The voice of doubt echoed in the vast space, mocking his efforts and questioning his faith.

"You have dedicated your life to the Almighty, but what have you truly accomplished? You are alone, your words falling on deaf ears."

Jameson closed his eyes, drawing strength from his faith. "I have served faithfully, not for recognition, but for the love of the Almighty and the hope of guiding others. My worth is not measured by numbers, but by the sincerity of my heart."

The cathedral filled with light, and he found himself surrounded by the supportive presence of his friends and congregation.

Father Benedict stood on the edge of a precipice, overlooking a churning sea of doubt and regret. The voices of those he had failed rang in his ears, their accusations cutting deep.

"You claim to be a man of faith, but where was your faith when it truly mattered?"

Benedict felt the weight of his guilt, but he stood firm. "I am flawed, as we all are, but I have never stopped seeking redemption and striving to be better. My journey is one of growth and forgiveness."

The precipice transformed into a solid, golden path, and he felt the reassuring presence of his friends beside him.

As each of the chosen ones faced their trials, they emerged stronger, their faith and unity reaffirmed. The ethereal landscape dissolved, and they found themselves back in the catacombs, the box containing the Eternal Echo glowing with a pure, radiant light.

The resonant voice spoke once more, filled with warmth and approval. "You have proven yourselves worthy. The Eternal Echo is now yours to wield. Use it wisely, for its power is great."

Reverend Jameson carefully lifted the box, feeling its weight and significance. "We will use it to protect our town and to ensure that the darkness never returns."

With the Eternal Echo in their possession, the chosen ones made their way back to Havenbrook, their hearts filled with a renewed sense of purpose and unity. The town welcomed them with open arms, the air alive with hope and gratitude.

As they stood together in the town square, the first rays of dawn breaking through the clouds, they knew that their journey was far from over. But with the light of the Almighty guiding them and the Eternal Echo in their hands, they were ready to face whatever challenges lay ahead.

The echoes of their trials would remain with them, a reminder of the strength and resilience they had found within themselves. And as they moved forward, united in their faith and commitment to the light, they knew that they could overcome any darkness, together.

13

The Judgment

Chapter 10:

The first light of dawn cast long shadows over Havenbrook as the chosen ones returned from their final confrontation. Exhaustion weighed heavily on their shoulders, but a newfound sense of peace and unity buoyed their spirits. The Divine Council's power had been shattered, and the whispers of the Almighty had led them to a decisive victory. Yet, an unspoken understanding lingered among them—they were not yet free from the trials of their journey.

Reverend Jameson and Emily stood at the church's entrance, watching the sun rise over the horizon. The golden light bathed the town in a warm glow, a stark contrast to the darkness they had faced. Father Benedict approached, his face lined with both relief and lingering concern.

"We've come so far," he said softly, "but I fear the final judgment is yet to come."

Emily nodded, her eyes scanning the peaceful town. "We need to prepare. The prophecies spoke of a reckoning, a test that would determine our fate."

Jameson turned to them, his expression resolute. "Gather everyone. We must face this together, as we always have."

By mid-morning, the chosen ones were assembled in the church, their faces reflecting a mixture of hope and apprehension. The air was thick with anticipation, as if the very walls of the ancient building were holding their breath.

Jameson stood before them, the Book of Prophecies in his hands. "We have faced many trials and emerged stronger for it," he began, his voice steady. "But the final judgment awaits. The Almighty will weigh our deeds and our hearts. We must be ready to face whatever comes."

As he spoke, a sudden chill swept through the room, extinguishing the candles and plunging them into darkness. The chosen ones gasped, their eyes straining to see in the dim light.

A low, resonant voice filled the air, echoing through the church. "You have come far, but the final test is upon you. Prepare yourselves for the judgment."

The voice seemed to come from everywhere and nowhere, its power palpable. The chosen ones exchanged nervous glances, their resolve tested by the unseen presence.

Suddenly, the ground beneath them trembled, and a blinding light filled the room. When the light subsided, they found themselves standing in a vast, ethereal landscape, unlike anything they had ever seen. The sky was a swirling tapestry of colors, and the ground was a shimmering expanse of light and shadow.

At the center of this otherworldly realm stood a figure, radiating an intense, divine energy. The figure's face was obscured by a brilliant halo, and its presence filled the chosen ones with a mixture of awe and fear.

"Welcome," the figure said, its voice resonating with an otherworldly power. "You stand before the Almighty for the final judgment."

Reverend Jameson stepped forward, his heart pounding in his chest. "We are ready to face the judgment," he said, his voice unwavering. "We have followed the path set before us and faced every trial with faith and unity."

The figure nodded, its halo pulsing with light. "You have indeed faced many trials, but the final test is one of the heart. Each of you must confront your deepest fears and darkest secrets. Only then can you truly be judged."

As the figure spoke, the landscape shifted and changed. Each of the chosen ones found themselves standing alone in a separate, isolated space, their surroundings reflecting their innermost fears.

Emily found herself in a dark, oppressive forest, the trees closing in around her. The whispers she had fought so hard to silence returned, louder and more insistent. She felt a presence behind her and turned to see a shadowy figure, its eyes glowing with malevolent intent.

"Do you think you can escape your past?" the figure hissed. "Do you think you are worthy of the Almighty's favor?"

Emily's heart raced, but she stood her ground. "I have faced my fears and my past," she said, her voice steady. "I am not perfect, but I have strived to do what is right."

The figure laughed, a cold, mocking sound. "We shall see," it said, before vanishing into the darkness.

Elsewhere, Jameson found himself standing before a vast, empty cathedral. The silence was deafening, and the weight of his responsibilities pressed down on him like a physical force. He heard a familiar voice and turned to see his late wife, her face filled with sadness.

"You have always put your duty before everything else," she said softly. "But what of your own heart? Have you truly lived, or have you merely existed?"

Jameson's eyes filled with tears. "I have tried to serve faithfully," he whispered. "But I have also made mistakes. I can only hope that my intentions were pure."

Father Benedict stood on a precipice, overlooking a churning sea of doubt and regret. He saw the faces of those he had failed, their accusations ringing in his ears. "You claim to be a man of faith, but where was your faith when it truly mattered?" they demanded.

Benedict clenched his fists, his heart aching with guilt. "I am flawed, as we all are," he said. "But I have never stopped striving to be better, to seek redemption."

As each of the chosen ones faced their personal trials, they realized that the judgment was not about perfection but about the journey, the struggle, and the growth they had experienced. One by one, they confronted their fears, confessed their sins, and affirmed their commitment to the path of light.

The ethereal landscape began to dissolve, and they found themselves back in the church, standing before the radiant figure. The figure's halo pulsed with a warm, golden light, and its voice was filled with a gentle power.

"You have faced the final test and revealed the truth of your hearts," the figure said. "The Almighty has seen your struggles, your failures, and your triumphs. You are not perfect, but you are worthy."

The chosen ones felt a wave of relief and gratitude wash over them. They had been judged not by their perfection but by their faith, their unity, and their willingness to confront their deepest fears.

The figure's light grew brighter, filling the church with a divine radiance. "Go forth with the knowledge that you are guided by the light of the Almighty. Your journey is not over, but you have proven your worth."

As the light faded, the chosen ones found themselves alone in the church once more, the dawn's light streaming through the stained glass windows. They looked at each other, their hearts filled with a renewed sense of purpose and unity.

They had faced the final judgment and emerged stronger for it. The path ahead would still be fraught with challenges, but they knew that they were not alone. The whispers of the Almighty would continue to guide them, and together, they would face whatever the future held, united in their faith and their commitment to the light.

14

The Whispering Shadows

The chosen ones returned to Havenbrook in the dead of night, the eerie stillness of the town starkly contrasting with the chaos they had left behind in the temple. The weight of their victory against the Divine Council hung heavily upon them, but a new sense of dread began to seep into their hearts. The shadows seemed to grow longer, and the whispers they had fought to silence echoed even louder in their minds.

Emily and Reverend Jameson stayed behind in the church, their faces lined with exhaustion and concern. The young woman they had saved rested on a pew, her breaths shallow and her eyes wide with fear. The night's events had left her shaken, and she clung to Emily for comfort.

"We must protect her," Jameson said, his voice low but resolute. "The Council will not give up so easily. They'll come for her again."

Emily nodded, her gaze fixed on the girl. "We need to keep her safe. And we need to find out more about the whispers. They're growing stronger."

Jameson agreed, but before they could plan further, a sudden chill filled the church. The candles flickered, and an unnatural darkness crept into the corners of the room. The whispers grew louder, an insidious murmur that seemed to seep into their very souls.

Emily stood, her heart pounding. "Do you hear that?" she asked, her voice barely above a whisper.

Jameson nodded, his expression grim. "The shadows... they're alive."

The two moved cautiously through the church, their lanterns casting weak beams of light that seemed to be swallowed by the encroaching darkness. The whispers grew louder, more distinct, as if they were surrounded by unseen entities.

"Beware the darkness," the whispers hissed. "Beware the shadows."

Emily felt a cold hand brush against her arm, and she jumped, nearly dropping her lantern. "What was that?" she gasped, her voice trembling.

Jameson held his lantern higher, illuminating the empty pews and the ancient stone walls. "We are not alone," he said. "The shadows are watching us."

Suddenly, the door to the church burst open, and Father Benedict rushed in, his face pale and his eyes wide with fear. "They're here!" he shouted. "The shadows have come alive!"

Before they could react, the darkness surged forward, enveloping the room in a suffocating shroud. The whispers became a cacophony, a chorus of malevolent voices that seemed to come from all directions.

"Run!" Jameson shouted, grabbing Emily's hand and pulling her towards the back of the church. Father Benedict followed, his steps faltering as the shadows clung to him, trying to drag him down.

They burst through a side door and into the night, the cold air biting at their skin. The darkness seemed to follow them, a living entity that pursued them through the deserted streets of Havenbrook.

"We need to find the others!" Emily shouted, her voice barely audible over the roar of the shadows. "We can't fight this alone!"

Jameson led them towards the center of town, where the rest of the chosen ones were likely hiding. They moved quickly, their lanterns flickering as the shadows pressed in around them. The whispers continued, now filled with mocking laughter and threats.

"You cannot escape us," they hissed. "The darkness is eternal."

As they reached the town square, they saw the others huddled together, their faces pale with fear. The shadows had surrounded them, a swirling mass of darkness that seemed impenetrable.

Jameson raised his lantern high, the light casting a weak glow that barely penetrated the darkness. "We have to stand together," he shouted. "The light will protect us!"

The chosen ones gathered around, their lanterns held high. The combined light pushed back the shadows, creating a small circle of safety in the midst of the darkness.

"We need to find the source," Emily said, her voice filled with determination. "There has to be something driving these shadows, something we can stop."

Father Benedict nodded. "The whispers... they spoke of a place. An ancient well, hidden in the forest. It's said to be a gateway to the underworld, a place where the darkness dwells."

Jameson's eyes widened. "The Well of Shadows," he said. "It's mentioned in the prophecies. If we can close it, we might be able to stop the shadows."

With no time to lose, the chosen ones set off towards the forest, the shadows nipping at their heels. They moved quickly, their lanterns lighting the way as they navigated the twisted paths and dense underbrush.

The whispers grew louder as they approached the well, a low, insidious chant that seemed to vibrate through the air. The forest itself seemed to come alive, the trees twisting and writhing as if possessed by the same dark force.

At last, they reached a clearing, where an ancient stone well stood. The air around it was thick with darkness, a swirling vortex of shadows that seemed to pulse with a malevolent energy.

"We have to seal it," Jameson said, his voice trembling. "We need to use the Book of Prophecies."

Father Benedict stepped forward, holding the book aloft. "The power of the Almighty will guide us," he said, his voice filled with conviction.

As he began to chant the ancient incantation, the shadows surged forward, their whispers becoming a deafening roar. The chosen ones formed a circle around the well, their lanterns casting a protective light that kept the darkness at bay.

The ground trembled, and a blinding light burst forth from the well, illuminating the forest with an otherworldly glow. The shadows recoiled, their whispers turning to screams as the light grew stronger.

With a final, powerful chant, Father Benedict thrust the book into the well. The light intensified, and the shadows were drawn into the vortex, their forms disintegrating as they were consumed by the divine power.

The forest fell silent, the whispers finally silenced. The chosen ones stood in stunned silence, their hearts pounding with relief and exhaustion. The well was sealed, and the darkness had been vanquished.

As they made their way back to Havenbrook, the first rays of dawn broke through the trees, casting a warm, golden light on the town. The whispers were gone, and the shadows had been driven back. But the chosen ones knew that their journey was far from over. The trials ahead would be no less daunting, but they were ready to face them, united in their faith and determination.

The light of the Almighty had guided them through the darkness, and they would continue to follow its path, no matter where it led.

15

The Final Revelation

The atmosphere in Havenbrook was thick with an oppressive tension as the chosen ones regrouped in the church. The whispers and shadows that had plagued them were gone, but a deeper unease lingered. They knew that the Divine Council had not been fully defeated, and a final confrontation loomed on the horizon. The air crackled with anticipation, as if the very town itself held its breath, waiting for what was to come.

Reverend Jameson, Emily, and Father Benedict stood at the altar, their faces lined with exhaustion and resolve. The ancient scrolls lay open before them, illuminated by the flickering candlelight. The Book of Prophecies, now marked by the battles they had fought, seemed to hum with a faint, otherworldly energy.

"We need to understand the final prophecy," Jameson said, his voice breaking the heavy silence. "The one that speaks of the ultimate test."

Emily nodded, her eyes scanning the scrolls. "There has to be a clue here, something we've missed."

Father Benedict's brow furrowed in concentration as he traced the symbols with his fingers. "The prophecies have always been obscure, but they've guided us this far. We must trust that the answers are here."

As they worked, the remaining chosen ones gathered around, their expressions reflecting a mixture of fear and determination. The church, once a sanctuary of peace, had become a war room, its sacred walls now witnesses to their struggle against the darkness.

Hours passed, the candles burning low, when Emily's eyes widened with sudden understanding. "Here," she said, pointing to a passage. "This speaks of a place where the veil between worlds is thinnest, where the divine and the mortal realms intersect. The final revelation will occur there."

Jameson leaned in, reading the passage aloud. "The place where the sun meets the earth, where shadows cannot hide. It is there that the true nature of the Almighty will be revealed, and the final test of faith will be faced."

Father Benedict's eyes lit up with recognition. "The plateau above the cliffs," he said. "It's the highest point in Havenbrook, where the sunrise first touches the land. That must be the place."

A murmur of agreement spread through the group. They quickly gathered their supplies, knowing that they had no time to lose. The final prophecy had to be confronted before the Divine Council could regroup and enact their own plans.

As dawn approached, they set out towards the cliffs, the early morning mist cloaking their path. The journey was steep and treacherous, the rocky terrain testing their endurance. But they pressed on, driven by the knowledge that their destiny awaited them at the summit.

When they reached the plateau, the first rays of sunlight were beginning to pierce the horizon, casting a golden glow over the land. The view was breathtaking, the entire town of Havenbrook spread out below them like a tapestry. But there was no time to admire the scenery. They had come for a purpose.

In the center of the plateau stood an ancient stone circle, its weathered pillars etched with symbols similar to those in the Book of Prophecies. The air was thick with a palpable energy, a sense that they stood on the threshold of something momentous.

The chosen ones formed a circle around the stones, their lanterns casting a warm light that mingled with the dawn. Jameson stepped forward, the Book of Prophecies held aloft. "We stand here, at the place of final revelation, to seek the truth and face the ultimate test of our faith."

As he spoke, the ground beneath them began to tremble, and a low hum resonated through the air. The pillars of the stone circle glowed with an inner light, and the air shimmered with a faint, golden haze.

Suddenly, a figure appeared in the center of the circle, materializing from the light. It was the stranger who had first arrived in Havenbrook, his presence as commanding and enigmatic as ever. But now, his eyes held a profound sadness, as if he bore the weight of the world's sorrow.

"You have done well to come this far," the stranger said, his voice carrying a resonance that seemed to vibrate through their very souls. "But the final test awaits. You must prove your faith and your unity, or all will be lost."

Emily stepped forward, her heart pounding. "What must we do?" she asked, her voice steady despite the fear that gripped her.

The stranger extended his hand, and the light intensified, forming a doorway of shimmering gold. "Beyond this door lies the truth of the Almighty and the heart of the Divine Council's power. You must enter together and face the darkness that resides there."

The chosen ones exchanged determined glances, their resolve hardening. They knew that this was the moment they had been preparing for, the culmination of their journey. With a collective breath, they stepped forward, crossing the threshold into the unknown.

On the other side, they found themselves in a vast, shadowy chamber, its walls lined with ancient runes that pulsed with a sinister energy. At the center stood a massive altar, upon which lay a crystal, glowing with a dark, ominous light.

The air was thick with an oppressive presence, and the whispers returned, louder and more insistent than ever. The shadows seemed to writhe and twist around them, taking on vaguely humanoid forms that watched with malevolent intent.

Reverend Jameson approached the altar, the Book of Prophecies in hand. "This is the heart of their power," he said, his voice echoing in the chamber. "We must destroy it."

Father Benedict nodded, his eyes fixed on the crystal. "But how? The power here is immense. We cannot simply break it."

Emily felt a sudden clarity, a sense of purpose that cut through the fear. "The book," she said. "It has guided us this far. It must hold the answer."

As Jameson opened the book, the pages glowed with a brilliant light. The symbols on the altar responded, their dark energy flickering and weakening. The chosen ones gathered around, their faith and unity forming a protective barrier against the encroaching darkness.

With a final, powerful incantation, Jameson raised the book high, and the light from its pages enveloped the crystal. The shadows screamed and writhed, their forms disintegrating in the face of the divine energy.

The crystal shattered, releasing a shockwave of light that filled the chamber. The darkness was banished, the whispers silenced. The chosen ones stood in stunned silence, their hearts pounding with the realization that they had succeeded.

As the light faded, the chamber transformed. The oppressive atmosphere lifted, replaced by a serene, golden glow. The stranger reappeared, his expression now one of peace and relief.

"You have proven yourselves," he said, his voice filled with gratitude. "The final revelation is complete. The power of the Divine Council is broken, and the truth of the Almighty is restored."

The chosen ones felt a profound sense of accomplishment and unity. They had faced the ultimate test and emerged victorious. As they returned to Havenbrook, the first rays of sunlight bathed the town in a new dawn, a symbol of the hope and light they had restored.

The journey had been arduous, the trials many, but their faith had carried them through. And as they stood together, the whispers of the Almighty now a gentle, guiding presence, they knew that they were ready to face whatever the future held, united in their purpose and their faith.

16

The Silent Messenger

The town of Havenbrook had always been a place where life moved slowly. Nestled in a valley surrounded by dense forests and rolling hills, it was a sanctuary of tranquility. Its residents were simple folk, their lives intertwined through generations of shared history and community bonds. The most exciting events were the annual harvest festival and the occasional out-of-town visitor. But all that changed one autumn evening when a stranger arrived, cloaked in mystery and whispers of the divine.

The first person to see him was old Mrs. Thompson, who lived alone in the last house on Maple Street. She was sitting on her porch, knitting a scarf for her grandson, when she noticed a figure emerging from the forest's edge. The man was tall, dressed in a long, dark coat that billowed around him in the evening breeze. His face was obscured by the wide brim of a hat, casting a shadow that seemed to swallow the fading light.

Mrs. Thompson watched as he walked with purpose down the road, pausing only once to glance around as if taking in his surroundings. His movements were smooth, almost ethereal, and for a moment, she felt a chill run down her spine. She shook her head, dismissing the unease as an old woman's fancy, and returned to her knitting.

The stranger continued his journey into the heart of Havenbrook, his presence unnoticed by most as they went about their evening routines. It wasn't until he reached the town square, where the statue of the town's founder stood proudly, that people began to take note. The square was bustling with activity as children played and parents chatted, but a hush fell over the crowd as he approached the statue.

He stopped at its base, looking up at the bronze figure with an intensity that drew the townsfolk's attention. Conversations ceased, and curious eyes turned towards him. The stranger raised his hand and pointed to the statue, his voice low but carrying a weight that demanded silence.

"I bring a message," he declared, his voice cutting through the evening air like a knife. "A message from the Almighty."

Gasps of shock and murmurs of disbelief rippled through the crowd. The man's claim was audacious, bordering on blasphemous in the eyes of some. Who was this stranger to speak for God? And why had he come to their quiet town?

Reverend Jameson, the town's pastor, stepped forward, his expression a mix of skepticism and concern. "What is this message you claim to bring?" he asked, his voice steady but wary.

The stranger turned his gaze towards the reverend, his eyes piercing and dark. "The Almighty has spoken to me," he replied. "And I am here to deliver His words. Change is coming. Prepare yourselves, for the days ahead will test your faith and your resolve."

The reverend frowned, his mind racing. "And why should we believe you? Many have come before, claiming to speak for God, only to lead people astray."

The stranger nodded, as if expecting the question. "You will believe, not because of my words, but because of what is to come. Watch for the signs, and you will see the truth."

With that, he turned and walked away, leaving the townsfolk in stunned silence. He disappeared into the night, his presence lingering like a shadow over Havenbrook.

The days that followed were filled with unease and speculation. Who was the stranger? Where had he come from? And what did his message mean? The people of Havenbrook were divided. Some dismissed him as a madman or a charlatan, while others felt a strange pull, a sense that something significant was indeed on the horizon.

Mrs. Thompson couldn't shake the feeling of foreboding that had settled over her since that evening. She found herself watching the forest edge, expecting to see the stranger reappear at any moment. Her nights were restless, filled with dreams of darkness and whispers she couldn't understand.

Reverend Jameson, too, was troubled. He spent long hours in his study, poring over scriptures and praying for guidance. He felt the weight of his responsibility to his congregation, and the stranger's words echoed in his mind. Was this a test of faith, as the stranger had suggested? Or was it a deception, meant to lead them away from the true path?

A week passed, and the town began to settle back into its routine, the stranger's visit fading into memory. But just as life seemed to return to normal, the first sign appeared.

It was a Sunday morning, and the townsfolk had gathered at the church for service. The pews were filled with familiar faces, all wearing expressions of reverence and anticipation. Reverend Jameson stood at the pulpit, preparing to deliver his sermon, when a sudden hush fell over the congregation.

A young boy, no more than ten years old, stood at the back of the church, his eyes wide with fear. "Fire," he whispered, his voice trembling. "There's a fire at the mill."

Panic erupted as the words sank in. The mill was the lifeblood of Havenbrook, its operation crucial to the town's economy. Without it, many would lose their livelihoods. People rushed out of the church, their faces pale with fear and dread.

When they reached the mill, they found the boy's words to be true. Flames licked at the wooden structure, smoke billowing into the sky. The townsfolk worked frantically to extinguish the fire, forming a human chain to pass buckets of water from the river. Despite their efforts, the fire raged on, relentless and unforgiving.

As they battled the blaze, a figure appeared on the hill overlooking the mill. It was the stranger, his coat and hat unmistakable. He watched silently, his presence once again sending a chill through those who saw him.

Reverend Jameson, covered in soot and sweat, looked up at the hill and saw the stranger. A sense of dread filled him, and he knew in his heart that this was the first sign the man had spoken of. The test had begun, and the people of Havenbrook were caught in the grip of a divine mystery that would change their lives forever.

Milton Keynes UK
Ingram Content Group UK Ltd.
UKHW020337050824
446478UK00015B/612